Star Gleams

Also from Westphalia Press

westphaliapress.org

Star Gleams

A Collection of Songs, Odes, and Ceremonials

by Carrie B. Jennings

WESTPHALIA PRESS
An imprint of Policy Studies Organization

Westphalia Press
An imprint of Policy Studies Organization
1527 New Hampshire Ave., NW
Washington, D.C. 20036
info@ipsonet.org

ISBN-13: 978-1633910287
ISBN-10: 1633910288

Cover design by Taillefer Long at Illuminated Stories:
www.illuminatedstories.com

Daniel Gutierrez-Sandoval, Executive Director
PSO and Westphalia Press

Devin Proctor, Director of Media and Publications
PSO and Westphalia Press

Updated material and comments on this edition
can be found at the Westphalia Press website:
www.westphaliapress.org

NINTH EDITION

Star Gleams

by

Carrie B. Jennings

Price 65 cents

:◦:

Quantity Prices upon Application.

PUBLISHED BY C. B. JENNINGS MUSIC CO.

HOWARD CITY, MICH.

.:.

Star Gleams

by

Carrie B. Jennings.

A Collection of
SONGS, ODES AND
CEREMONIALS

for

Eastern Star Chapters *of the* World

Dedicated to the
GENERAL GRAND CHAPTER, O.E.S.
Convening in SEATTLE, WASHINGTON, — July, 1919
AND
TO MRS. EMMA C. OCOBOCK OF MICHIGAN,
MOST WORTHY GRAND MATRON.

Price 65¢
Quantity prices upon application.
Published by C. B. Jennings Music Co.,
HOWARD CITY, MICH.

CONTENTS

America

SAMUEL FRANCIS SMITH   HENRY CAREY

1. My country! 'tis of thee, Sweet land of liberty,
2. My native country! thee, Land of the noble free,
3. Let music swell the breeze, And ring from all the trees
4. Our Father's God! to thee, Author of liberty!

Of thee I sing: Land where my fathers died, Land of the
Thy name I love; I love thy rocks and rills, Thy woods and
Sweet freedom's song;— Let mortal tongues a-wake, Let all that
To thee we sing; Long may our land be bright, With freedom's

Pil-grims' pride, From ev-'ry mountain side Let freedom ring!
tem-pled hills; My heart with rapture thrills, Like that a-bove.
breathe par-take; Let rocks their silence break, The sound pro-long.
ho-ly light Protect us by thy might, Great God our King.

Tune America

1. God bless our Eastern Star,
   Long may its beams afar
   Shed their bright light;
   Emblem of love and truth
   Patron of age and youth
   In every grace, forsooth
   Thy beams unite.

2. When the deep shadows fall
   Thy rays encompass all
   Glad Eastern Star;
   And in our festal hour
   Own we thy quickening power;
   Of strength a mighty tower,
   Oh, Eastern Star

Star Gleams

The Star-Spangled Banner

FRANCIS SCOTT KEY. 1814

Solo or Quartet

1. Oh,— say, can you see, by the dawn's ear-ly light, What so
2. On the shore dim-ly seen thro' the mists of the deep, Where the
3. Oh,— thus be it ev-er when free-men shall stand Be-

proud-ly we hailed at the twi-light's last gleam-ing, Whose broad stripes and bright
foe's haugh-ty host in dread si-lence re-pos-es, What is that which the
tween their loved home and wild war's des-o-la-tion, Blest with vic-t'ry and

stars, thro' the clouds of the fight, O'er the ram-parts we watched, were so
breeze, o'er the tow-er-ing steep, As it fit-ful-ly blows, half con-
peace, may the heav'n res-cued land Praise the Pow'r that hath made and pre-

gal - lant ly - stream-ing? And the rock-ets' red glare, the bombs burst-ing in
ceals, half dis - clos - es? Now it catch-es the gleam of the morn-ing's first
served us a na - tion! Then_ con-quer we must, when our cause it is

air, Gave_ proof thro' the night that our flag was still there.
beam, In full glo - ry re - flect - ed now shines on the stream:
just, And_ this be our mot - to: "In God is our trust!"

CHORUS

Oh_ say does that_ star span-gled ban - ner _ yet _
Tis the star span - gled_ ban - ner oh long may _ it _
And the star span-gled_ ban - ner in tri - umph_ shall_

cresc. *ff*

wave_ O'er the land_ of the free and the home of the brave?
wave_ O'er the land_ of the free and the home of the brave!
wave_ O'er the land_ of the free and the home of the brave.

Star Gleams

Battle Hymn of the Republic

JULIA WARD HOWE   Air: "JOHN BROWN'S BODY"

Allegretto

1. Mine eyes have seen the glo-ry of the com-ing of the Lord; He is
2. I have seen Him in the watch-fires of a hun-dred cir-cling camps; They have
3. I have read a fier-y gos-pel writ in bur-nished rows of steel; "As ye
4. He has sound-ed forth the trump-et that shall nev-er call re-treat; He is
5. In the beau-ty of the lil-ies Christ was born a-cross the sea; With a

tramp-ing out the vint-age where the grapes of wrath are stored; He hath
build-ed Him an al-tar in the eve-ning dews and damps; I can
deal with my con-tem-ners, so with you my grace shall deal." Let the
sift-ing out the hearts of men be-fore His judg-ment seat; O be
glo-ry in His bos-om that trans-fig-ures you and me; As He

loosed the fate-ful light-ning of His ter-ri-ble swift sword, His truth is march-ing on.
read His right-eous sen-tence by the dim and flar-ing lamps, His day is march-ing on.
He-ro, born of wom-an, crush the ser-pent with His heel, Since God is march-ing on.
swift, my soul, to an-swer Him! be ju-bi-lant, my feet! Our God is march-ing on.
died to make men ho-ly, let us die to make men free, While God is march-ing on.

CHORUS

Glo-ry! glo-ry! Hal-le-lu-jah! Glo-ry! glo-ry! Hal-le-lu-jah!

Glo-ry! glo-ry! Hal-le-lu-jah! His truth is march-ing on.

Star Gleams

Onward Christian Soldiers

S. BARING-GOULD

A. S. SULLIVAN

On-ward, Chris-tian sol-diers! March-ing as to war, With the cross of
Like a might-y ar-my Moves the Church of God Broth-ers we are
Crowns and thorns may per-ish, King-doms rise and wane, But the Church of
On-ward, then ye faith-full Join our hap-py throng, Blend with ours your

Je - sus Go-ing on be - fore: Christ, the roy - al Mas - ter,
tread - ing Where the saints have trod; We are not di - vid - ed,
Je - sus Con-stant will re - main; Gates of hell can nev - er
voic - es In the tri - umph song; Glo - ry, praise, and hon - or

Leads a-gainst the foe; For-ward in-to bat - tle See. His ban-ners go!
All one bod - y we, One in hope and doc - trine, One in char-i - ty.
'Gainst that Church pre - vail; We have Christ's own prom-ise, And that can-not fail.
Un - to Christ the King, This thro' count less a - ges Men and an-gels sing.

CHORUS

On-ward, Chris-tian sol - diers! March-ing as to war,

With the cross of Je - sus Go - ing on be - fore.

Star Gleams

8

Rally Round The Standard
Rallying Song
Written for the Montcalm- Mecosta County Association 1919
Mrs. Nora B. Musson, President

Adapted by CARRIE B. JENNINGS

H. C. WORK

With spirit

Ral - ly round the stand-ard sis - ters, Pass the word a - long
At the call of gav - el nev - er let your ar - dor lag;
Ral - ly round the stand-ard sis - ters, Pass the word a - long

Of a grand as - sem-blage form-ing Man - y thou-sand strong_____
Ev - er fore-most in the van we'll raise our star - ry flag,_____
In this day of glad re - joic - ing Lift your voice in song,_____

Sol - diers of the East - ern Star, A vast and hap - py throng
Let no gold - en mo - ments pass Nor let your col - ors drag,
Daugh - ters of The East - ern Star, The joy - ful notes pro - long

Swell-ing the ranks of our or - der.
Seek - ing the good of the or - der.
Sound-ing the praise of our or - der.　　The Star, The Star, A

song of glad - ness raise, The Star, The Star, with

notes of lof - ty praise _____ Daugh-ters of the East-ern Star, Re-

flect her sil - ver rays sound - ing the praise of our or - der.

Star Gleams

Columbia, the Gem of the Ocean

D. T. SHAW   THOMAS A. BECKET

Spirited

O   Co - lum - bia,   the gem   of   the   o - cean,   The __
When __   war winged   its wide des - o - la - tion,   And __
The __   Star span - gled ban - ner   bring hith - er,   O'er Co -

home of the brave __ and the   free, __   The __ shrine of each pa - triot's de -
threat-ened the land __ to de - form, __   The __ ark then of free - dom's foun -
lum - bia's true sons __ let it   wave;   May the wreaths they have won nev - er

vo - tion,   A __   world __ of - fers hom - age to   thee.   Thy __
da - tion,   Co -   lum - bia, rode safe __ thro' the storm: With the
with - er,   Nor its   stars __ cease to shine __ on the brave: May the

man-dates make he - roes as - sem - ble,   When __   Lib - er - ty's form stands in
gar - lands of vic - t'ry a - round her,   When so   proud - ly she bore __ her brave
ser - vice, u - nit - ed ne'er sev - er,   But __   hold to their col - ors so

Star Gleams

OPENING

Oh Eastern Star

C. B. J.

CARRIE B. JENNINGS

Oh East-ern Star, bright East-ern Star, We love thy shin ing - light, We
Oh East-ern Star, bright East-ern Star, Once more we sing thy praise, And

love the pre-cepts sym-bolled In thy col-ors fair and bright. We
once a-gain pro-tec-tion seek, 'Neath thy in-spir-ing rays, And

love the true and faith-ful blue, Thy sheaf of gold-en maize, The
once a-gain our vows en-shrine, And plight our faith a-new; Once

white so pure, the ten-der green, The red and fer-vant rays.
more in-voke the Pow'r di-vine, To keep us ev-er true.

Star Gleams

Ode
(Tune Maryland, My Maryland)

CARRIE B. JENNINGS   Mrs. JANE W. BRENT

Star of The East, we sing to thee, East-ern Star, glad East-ern Star;
Thou had'st thy birth on hal-lowed ground, East-ern Star, oh, East-ern Star;
Thy vir-tues are our strength and pride, East-ern Star, oh, East-ern Star;

Thy truths in all a-round we see, East-ern Star, bright East-ern Star;
And light and glo-ry shone a-round, East-ern Star, proud East-ern Star;
Thy pre-cepts ev-er shall a-bide, East-ern Star, bright East-ern Star;

Where-'er thou shed'st thy sil-ver light Thy sons and daugh-ters there u-nite
And ev-er shall thy beams re-call That cry of want or or-phan's call
Thy sil-ver rays must e'er be-speak De-feat of wrong, de-fense of weak,

To rat-i-fy each sa-cred rite, East-ern Star, oh East-ern Star.
May not by us un-heed-ed fall. East-ern Star, bright East-ern Star.
Thy hon-or may we ev-er seek East-ern Star, our East-ern Star.

Star Gleams

Heav'nly Father, Grant We Pray

C. B. J.

CARRIE B. JENNINGS

Heav'n-ly Fa-ther grant we pray Bless-ing on our work to day
Source of wis-dom let Thy light Guide our wand-'ring steps a - right

While we bow as sup-pliants here plight-ing our vows sin - cere
Trust-ing ev - er in Thy might God of the East-ern Star our Fa-ther

Let the smile of love di-vine From Thy face in - ra-diance shine
Thine the power and glo - ry be Ev - 'ry good we have from Thee

While we're wait-ing, con - se-crat - ing our bless-ed East-ern Star.
While we're wait-ing, con - se-crat - ing. God bless our East-ern Star.

OPENING

Once Again We Meet Together

C. B. J.

CARRIE B. JENNINGS

Once a-gain we meet to-geth-er In our chap-ter room
Once a-gain we pledge each oth-er Loy-al-ty sin-cere

Grate-ful hearts and smil-ing fa-ces Ban-ish care and gloom ___ shall ban-ish
Sym-pa-thy in ev-'ry tri-al Com-fort love and cheer ___ fra-ter-nal

shall ban-ish
fra-ter-nal

Once a-gain to God our Fa-ther come with songs of praise
Balm for ev-'ry wound-ed spir-it ev-'ry trou-bled heart

For His lov-ing Kind-ness which has crowned our ___ days.
Seek-ing help di-vine that each sus-tain (her) (his) ___ part.

Star Gleams

OPENING

Once More Love Fraternal Calls

Air. Belle Mahone

C . B . J.

J . H . Mc NAUGHTON

Once more love fra - ter - nal calls; Once a - gain in
Heav'n - ly Fa - ther give us light, Bless the vows that

chap - ter halls Greet we now with heart - y cheer
here we plight, Grant us strength to live a - right

All as - sem - bled here ___ While our du - ties
For our East - ern Star ___ Bound by hon - or's

we ful - fil Ban - ish ev - ry thought of ill,
sa - cred thrall, Faith - ful aye to du - ty's call,
Let true grace our hearts in - stil From our East - ern Star
Loy - al, trust-ful, lov - ing all In our East - ern Star
From our East - ern Star Glo - rious East - ern Star
In our East - ern Star Glo - rious East - ern Star
Let true grace our hearts in - stil From our East - ern Star
Loy - al, trust - ful lov - ing all In our East - ern Star

When Daylight Is Fading

C. B. J.   CARRIE B. JENNINGS

When day-light is fad-ing and night shad-ows creep, When the
Se - cure in thy pres-ence we lin - ger to-night, With

voic - es of na - ture are si - lent in sleep, Whence
hearts full of love for the truth and the right; Oh

com - eth the sil - ver light pierc - ing the gloom, Il-
guide us and help us that we, day by day May

lum - ing with beau - ty Our lov'd chap - ter room?
scat - ter the star - beams On life's toil - some way.

CHORUS

Our bright East - ern Star Our lov'd East - ern Star We

wel - come thy guid - ing light shin - ing a - far; No

clouds veil the sky where thy beams are re - leased Thou

ra - di - ant, won - der - ful Star of The East

Star Gleams

Once More In Our Chapter Room Meeting

C. B. J.   Air 'BONNIE

Once more in our chap-ter room meet-ing ___ Glad
Bid dis-cord and en-mi-ty van-ish ___ Dis-

hearts and glad voic-es we raise ___ In meas-ures of
pel ev-'ry shad-ow of gloom ___ Each thorn from our

sis-ter-ly greet-ing ___ And an-thems of heart-i-est praise ___
pres-ence we'll ban-ish ___ And bid on-ly ros-es to bloom ___

CHORUS

Meet-ing, greet-ing, send-ing the beams of our love a-far;

Glad hours fleet-ing, At home in our own East-ern Star ___

Star Gleams

OPENING

When Sailing on Life's Ocean

C. B. J.

Air SOLDIERS FAREWELL
KINKEL

When sail-ing on life's o-cean Mid bil-lows' wild com-
Do storms of grief op-press thee? Do fear and doubt pos-

mo - tion, Though storms your bark are rend - ing, Tem-
sess thee? The dark - ness is but seem - ing For

pes - tu-ous gales de - scend-ing Look up sad heart be
al - tar fires are gleam-ing Through dark - est night they

hold a - far A bea - con light,_ our East - ern Star
shine a - far The light of our_ bright East - ern Star

Star Gleams

OPENING

In the Turmoil of Life

Air BELIEVE ME IF ALL THOSE ENDEARING
YOUNG CHARMS

TOM MOORE

C. B. J.

In the tur - moil of life when the
Oh, blest Star of The East, there's no

wind and the gale In their surg - es en - gulf our frail
cloud in our sky That your sil - ver ray can - not dis -

bark, __ When the bil - lows dash high and dis - man - tled the sail, And no
pel, __ There's no gale of mis - for - tune we may not de - fy And no

ray seems to fath-om the dark __ Then my sis-ters take heart, there's a
rage that your love may not quell __ So to-geth-er we come and a

ha - ven close by And a ref-uge is sure-ly at
bless-ing we claim For our sis-ter-hood no-ble and

hand __ For the Star of The East sets her
grand __ With a faith firm-ly fixed in One

watch tower on high And will faith-ful-ly guide us to land.__
ev-er the same And Who hold-eth the world in His hand.__

Star Gleams

Beautiful Star

Adapted from "STAR OF THE EVENING"
by C. B. JENNINGS

1. Beau - ti - ful Star so pure and bright, Shed on us fra -
2. Shine on___ shine on and let thy ray Light the trav ler

ter - nal light; Send the beams of thy love a - far Star of The East our
on his way Point to the heav - en - ly gates a - jar Star of The East our

CHORUS

beau - ti - ful Star, Star of The East our beau - ti - ful Star Beau - ti - ful
beau - ti - ful Star, Star of The East our beau - ti - ful Star Beau - ti - ful

Star,___ Beau - ti - ful Star,___ Star of The
Star of The East

beau - ti - ful Star beau - ti - ful Star

East___ our beau - ti - ful, beau - ti - ful Star.___
Star of the East

Our, East - ern Star

OPENING

Within Our Chapter Walls

C. B. J.

CARRIE B. JENNINGS

Within our chapter walls once more we ___ meet, With love fraternal here once more to ___ greet So welcome all that makes that love complete And banish thoughts of ill.

May love and charity abide with us here And Martha's simple faith drive out all ___ fear Obedience constancy and courage clear adorn our Eastern Star.

Star Gleams

CLOSING
Good-Night

Adapted from OLD SCHOOL SONG
by CARRIE B. JENNINGS

Once more the happy evening's close
A fond farewell before we part

Brings the hour of sweet repose; Good night A-
Breathing love from heart to heart; Good night As

gain fraternal love we vow, Again in
forth we go where duties wait Our path we

song unite And seek God's blessing on our
may not see Yet in God's promise we a-

way As once more we softly say "Good-night."
bide As we say at eventide "Good-night."

Star Gleams

Sisters Dear, The Hour Has Come For Closing

Adapted from CHEER, BOYS, CHEER

C. B. J.

H. RUSSELL

1. Sis - ters dear, The hour has come for clos - ing
2. Sis - ters dear, In this our hour of part - ing

Sis - ters dear, Let all u - nite in sing - ing

CHORUS D. C.

Once more we go forth to the task of life With prob - lems new and
As we re - view the mer - cies of the day With hope in - spired up -

Prais - es to Him whose prom - is - es are sure, On the air in

du - ties fresh im - pos - ing With cour - age gained we en - ter on the strife.
on new du - ties start - ing The Star of Beth' - lem shines up - on our way.

hap - py ca - dence ring - ing To Him whose mer - cy ev - er shall en - dure.

Strength ened a - new by words of friend - ly greet - ing
Sure - ly with such a light our foot - steps guid - ing

Yet know - ing not what dan - gers wait be - fore, Still ev - 'ry heart in
Naught do we miss to make the path way clear While in the arms of

D.C. al Fine

con - fi - dence is beat - ing That strength will come to con - quer ev - er more
per - fect love a - bid - ing The per - fect love that cast - eth out all fear

Star Gleams

CLOSING

Now Once Again

C. B. J.   Air LOVES OLD SWEET SONG

Now once a-gain our chap-ter room we leave, Treas-ured with love the
May we like A - dah keep our hon - or bright; Like Ruth be firm in

truths we here re-ceive; Oh, may these les-sons help from day to day
con - stan - cy and right; Fear-less, like Es - ther, right-eous cause to plead;

Strength-en and guide our steps a - long life's way, So shall our or - der
Trust ful like Mar - tha in the hour of need, Strong like E - lec - ta;

stand be-fore the world Strong, with fra-ter-nal ban-ner broad un-furled.
and at sis-ter's call Char - i - ty lend, the crown-ing grace of all.

Star Gleams

CHORUS

Just a song at part-ing Just a fond good-night

Just a last re-new-al ___ Of the vows we plight

May no breath of e-vil ___ Our al-le-giance scar Liv-ing by the

pre-cepts Of our bright Star Our bright_ East-ern Star.

Star Gleams

CLOSING
Our Loving Heavenly Father

C. B. J.

CARRIE B JENNINGS

Our loving Heav'n-ly Father Thy bless-ing we im-
Oh be Thy pres-ence near us And grant from day to

plore As we go forth to life's du - ties From our
day Thy great heart shall en - dear us And

chap - ter home once more Oh may Thy pres - ence
help us to o - bey The pre - cepts Thou hast

light us O'er life's tem - pes - tu-ous sea And
giv - en; And prove wher - e'er we are That

Thy great love u - nite us in true fra - ter - ni - ty.
He who reigns in heav - en is with our East-ern Star. A - men.

Star Gleams

God Be With You
Till We Meet Again

CLOSING

T. E. RANKIN D.D.

W. G. TOMER

1. God be with you till we meet a - gain,
2. God be with you till we meet a - gain,
3. God be with you till we meet a - gain,
4. God be with you till we meet a - gain,

By His coun-sels guide, up - hold you, With His sheep se-cure-ly
'Neath His wings pro-tect-ing hide you, Dai - ly man-na still pro-
When life's per - ils thick con - found you, Put His arms un - fail-ing
Keep love's ban - ner float-ing o'er you, Smite death's threatening wave be -

fold you, God be with you till we meet a - gain.
vide you, God be with you till we meet a - gain.
round you, God be with you till we meet a - gain.
fore you, God be with you till we meet a - gain.

Till we meet, _____ till we meet, _____ Till we

Till we meet, till we meet, till we meet,

meet at Je - sus feet; Till we meet, _____ till we

Till we meet, Till we meet, till we

meet, _____ God be with you till we meet a - gain.

meet, till we meet.

Star Gleams

CLOSING
As The Happy Evening Closes
Tune: "Far Away"

C. B. J.   Mrs. J. W. BLISS

As the hap - py eve - ning clos - es And the time to part has come, Dreams of
Then good-night and pleas-ant dreaming Hap-py mem-o-ries will cling;   So - cial

rest the hour im - pos - es And the thought of "Home, sweet home."
hours with glad-ness teem - ing, All too swift - ly on the wing.

Turn the page and close the book   On the day that now is past,   Fa - ces
Let the part-ing hour be bright,   Know-ing not what lies be - yond,   But se -

turn to new be - gin - nings, Mak-ing foot - prints that shall last,   Write up -
cure in the as - sur - ance Of a strong fra - ter - nal bond,   Rest-ing

on   the fu - ture's pag - es Les - sons that shall tru - ly last.
in   the blest as - sur - ance Of a strong fra - ter - nal bond.

Star Gleams

Song of Welcome

Tune, Soldiers on Life's Battlefield

Welcome To Candidates.

CARRIE B. JENNINGS

Spirited

Wel - come, wel - come to our chap-ter room, — Wel - come to our
Wel - come, wel - come in our or - der bright, — Here new pleas-ures

or - der grand — Here new du-ties you as - sume, Clasp the glad fra - ter-nal hand.
rare un-fold — Joy and du - ty here u - nite Bound by links of pur-est gold.

Welcome, wel-come to our or - der Greet we as you hith - er come, _____
Welcome, wel-come to our or - der Let the greet-ing sound a - far, _____

Friend-ships find with - in the bor - der Of our lov'd fra - ter - nal home.
Safe - ty claim with - in the bor - der Of the glo - rious East-ern Star.

Published by
C. B. JENNINGS MUSIC CO.
Howard City, Mich.

Star Gleams

Eastern Star Ode

CARRIE B. JENNINGS

Adapted to use in the labyrinth
Air LEAD KINDLY LIGHT

1 Oh East-ern Star, that shed'st thy ho - ly light_____
2 And ev - en though we walk thru pas - tures green,
3 Fair A - dah viewed the sac - ri - fi - cial flame,_____
4 Dear East-ern Star, shed still thy ho - ly light_____
5 And thus may we re-flect thy beau - teous light_____

On life's dark__ way, ____ To guide the wear - y trav-'ler thru the
By wa - ters__ still,____ Not less may thy pro-tect-ing ray se -
Yet dared o - bey; ____ Sweet Ruth, tho hum - ble bears a death-less
Up - on our__ way ____ Thy al - tar fires il-lume our dark - est
Fair East - ern__ Star, ____ God grant we keep thy 'scut-cheon ev - er

night _____   Till breaks the day, _____   Shine on shine
rene _____   Keep us from ill. _____   And grant no
name _____   In thy pure ray. _____   Per - sia's proud
night _____   Our guide by day. _____   En - vy and
bright _____   To shine a - far. _____   May cour - age,

on, _____ and let thy sil - ver _____ gleam _____
act _____ of ours may dim _____ thy _____ spark, _____
queen, _____ E - lec - ta stanch and _____ true, _____
strife _____ thy ra - diance e'er _____ dis - pel _____
truth _____ and loy - al - ty _____ e'er _____ prove _____

Light us _____ thru _____ thorn - y path or tur - bid stream.
Our star _____ tho _____ skies be bright or clouds _____ be dark. _____
And Mar - tha's _____ faith all blend in thy _____ bright hue. _____
In love _____ fra - ter - nal let us ev _____ er dwell. _____
Our sis - ter - hood in char - it - 'ty _____ and love. _____

Star Gleams

Sweet Hour of Prayer

Rev. W. W. WALFORD, 1846   Wᵐ B. BRADBURY, 1859

1 Sweet hour of prayer, sweet hour of prayer, That calls me from a world of care, And bids me at my Father's throne Make all my wants and wishes known;

D. C. And oft escaped the tempter's snare, By thy return, sweet hour of prayer, And oft escaped the tempter's snare, By thy return, sweet hour of prayer!

In seasons of distress and grief, My soul has often found relief;

Sweet hour of prayer! sweet hour of prayer!
Thy wings shall my petition bear
To Him whose truth and faithfulness
Engage the waiting soul to bless.
And since He bids me seek His face
Believe His word, and trust His grace.
    I'll cast on Him my every care
And wait for thee, sweet hour of prayer

Sweet hour of prayer! sweet hour of prayer!
May I thy consolation share,
Till, from Mount Pisgah's lofty height,
I view my home and take my flight:
This robe of flesh I'll drop, and rise
To seize the everlasting prize:
    And shout, while passing through the air,
Farewell, farewell, sweet hour of prayer!

Blest Be The Tie That Binds

Dennis

1 Blest be the tie that binds
2 Be - fore our Fa - ther's throne,
3 We share our mu - tual woes,
4 When we a - sun - der part

Our hearts in Chris - tian love;
We pour our ar - dent prayers;
Our mu - tual bur - dens bear;
It gives us in - ward pain;

The fel - low - ship of kin - dred
Our fears our hopes our aims are
And oft - en for each oth - er
But we shall still be joined in

minds Is like to that a - bove.
one, Our com - forts and our cares.
flows The sym - pa - thiz - ing tear.
heart, And hope to meet a - gain.

Star Gleams

Installation

C. B. J.

Air OLD COLLEGE GLEE
Vive L'Amour

Play in march time

1. *Worthy Matron.* Come Sis-ters and Broth-ers and join in our lay,
2. *Worthy Patron.* All hail to the Pa-tron our guard-ian and guide,
3. *Associate Matron.* All hail to the West in its beau-ty en-rolled,
4. *Associate Patron.* All hail to the Ma-son who sits in the West, As
5. *Secretary.* All hail to the Scribe who our re-cord shall keep,
6. *Treasurer.* All hail to our Treas-ur-er hon-est, and true,

Hail to the glo-ri-ous East!— All hail to the Ma-tron we
Hail to the tie___ that binds!— All hail to the Pa-tron we
Hail to the gold-en West!— A help for our Ma-tron, her
so-ci-ate Pa-tron fine!— The badge of his of-fice his
Hail to the wor-thy Scribe!— Whose watch-ful vig-i-lance
Knight of the gold-en key!— Who safe guards our cash all the

wel-come to day, Hail to the sa-cred East!___
wel-come with pride, Hail to the tie___ that binds!___
hands to up hold, Hail to the gold-en West!___
worth will at-test, His func-tion it will___ de-fine!___
nev-er may sleep, Hail to the pa-tient Scribe!___
bus-y year through, Knight of the gold-en key!___

Joy - ful we greet her and heart - i - ly cheer ____
He is the link that con - nects our bright Star With
Bright the ef - ful - gent sun beams on our sight, With
His to shed rad - i - ance gleam - ing a - far, ____
Keep - ing the scroll where - up - on all may read With
True to the trust which with her we in - vest, ____

Queen of the gav - el for all the bright year __ Pledg - ing our loy - al - ty
or - ders ma-son - ic a - near and a - far Our bond of cre - den - tial at
lus - tre un-dimmed may this em-blem of light __ Shine with true mean-ing through
Shin - ing and clear as the crys-tal-ized spar, __ Guid-ance and light from the
grat - i - fied pride ev - ry sis - ter's good deed, __ Help - ing her chap - ter to
Fill - ing her sta - tion with busi-ness like zest, __ That thus her chap - ter may

true and sin - cere ____ Hail to the sov - 'reign East. ____
ma - son - ry's bar, ____ Hail to the tie that binds! ____
liv - ing a right, ____ Hail to the gold - en West ! ____
sym - bol - ized Star, As - so - ci - ate Pa - tron fine. ____
thrive and suc - ceed, ____ Hail to the no - ble Scribe. ____
not be dis - tressed, ____ Knight of the gold - en key! ____

Continued Page 40

Star Gleams

Installation (Continued)

7. CONDUCTRESSES

All hail the Conductresses, next in the line,
    Knights of baton and scroll;
Direction and discipline theirs to combine
    Symbol of wise control;
Entering candidates first they address,
Kind words of wise admonition express,
Meanings with permanence strive to impress;
    Knights of baton and scroll!

8. CHAPLAIN

Sweet Hour of Prayer   Page 36

9. MARSHAL

All hail to the Marshal so stately and fine
    Hail to the Marshal grand;
In all ceremonials given to shine,
    Graceful and calm and bland;
Mistress of courtesies when we convéne,
Conducting and serving with dignified mien,
Of form and good order a virtual queen,
    Hail to the Marshal Grand.

10. ORGANIST

Our worthy Organist gladly we greet,
    Goddess of lute and lyre.
Her tuneful service, with graces replete
    Harmony must inspire.
Whether we revel in sportive delight;
Or songs of the Order our voices unite;
Lending a charm to each sanctified rite
    Goddess of lute and lyre.

11. STAR POINTS

All hail to the rays of our beautiful Star
    Center of beauty bright;
Adorning our order and sending afar
    Beams of the morning light;
Bright in the beauty of colors most rare,
Bestowing in language of blossoms so fair,
Pleasures abounding for others to share
    Hail to The Eastern Star!

12. WARDER AND SENTINEL

Behold the Warder, who peace must maintain
    Intrusion she shall forestall;
Our Sentinel too, the last link in our chain
    Guard of the outer hall;
On their protection we confident lean
Secure in the strength of their vigilance keen
By them every act of intrusion foreseen,
    Welcome them one and all.

Memorial

Written for Mrs. C. Anna Greene
Chairman Obituary Committee
Golden Jubilee Session Michigan Grand Chapter O.E.S.
Detroit October 1917, by Carrie B. Jennings.

Into the realm of that unknown Vast
  Beyond the golden portal,
Out of the turmoil of earth they passed
  To dwell with the grand immortal.

It matters not that the forms we knew
  Lie silently, restfully sleeping,
We know that the hearts that for us beat true
  Are safe in the Master's keeping.

The brush of their garments, a vision of light,
  The touch of their soul's unveiling,
Like the breath of the lillies so pure and white
  From censers unseen exhaling.

The flowers may fade and their petals fall
  To enrich the soil with their sweetness,
But the breath of their fragrance is over all;
  They bloom in their full completeness

In a better, a fairer, a holier place
  Where death and decay come never;
Tomorrow they'll greet us, and face to face
  We shall live and shall love forever.

In the bright fields of Eden, our lillies fair
  Shall rival the stars of the morning;
And the King in His beauty shall find them there
  The home of His blessed adorning.

And may it not be in the mansions of bliss
  Which there for God's children are builded,
Which need not the sun, nor the moonbeams' kiss,
  By the light of His countenance gilded.

That these, the pure in heart, that day
  Shall give thanks to their Great High Priest
Saying: "Lord, by Thy mercy we found Thy way,
  For we saw Thy Star in The East."

Memorial

CARRIE B. JENNINGS

Tune THE VACANT CHAIR

1. From our chap-ter room we miss them, Loved ones
2. There no more shall storm clouds gath-er Ship-wrecked

who have gone be - fore But they wait to give us
lives shall be un - known For a lov - ing Heav'n-ly

wel-come O - ver on the oth - er shore, From our
Fath - er Ev - er - more shall guard his own, And the

songs we miss their voi - ces Miss the clasp of lov - ing
ha - ven seem - eth near - er For the loved ones gone be -

hands We have watched their bark sail home-ward, Drift-ing
fore They have made our star-beams clear-er Bea-cons

o-ver gold-en sands; Nev-er more our lips shall
on the oth-er shore; There where sor-row com-eth

greet them Till for us lifes voyage is past And with them we're safe-ly
nev-er Shel-tered from each chill-ing blast Where death's hand no ties may

an-chored In Our Fa-ther's home at last.
sev-er We shall gath-er home at last. Safe at last Home at last.

Star Gleams

Funerals
Cast Thy Burden On The Lord

OLD ANTHEM

Cast thy bur-den on the Lord, Cast thy bur-den on the Lord,

Cast thy bur-den on the Lord, Cast thy bur-den on the

Lord, And He will sus-tain thee and strength-en thee and com-fort thee

He will sus-tain thee and__ com-fort thee. He will sus-tain thee and__

com - fort thee. He will sus -tain thee, He__ will com-fort thee,

ritard

Cast thy bur - den on__ the Lord, Cast thy bur - den on__ the Lord.

Star Gleams

Funerals
Consolation

C. B. J.

CARRIE B. JENNINGS

1. Wea - ry heart with sor - row bowed place thy faith a - bove,
2. Let thy heart un - troub - led be, He who know - eth best

Lift thine eyes be - yond the cloud To the realms of love,
In the man - y man - sions free Builds a place of rest,

He who to the strick - en lamb Tem - pers ev - 'ry gale
Safe with - in His shelt - ring arms Nev - er more to roam,

Mark - ing e'en the spar - row's fall, His chil - dren will not fail.
Far re - moved from earth's a - larms A Fa - ther calls them home.

Star Gleams

Abide With Me
(Eventide)

HENRY F. LYTE   WILLIAM H. MONK

A - bide with me! Fast falls the e - ven tide,
Swift to its close ebbs out life's lit - tle day;
I need Thy pres - ence ev - 'ry pass - ing hour,
Hold Thou Thy cross be fore my clos - ing eyes;

The ___ dark - ness deep - ens, Lord, with me a - bide!
Earth's ___ joys grow dim, its glo - ries pass a - way;
What ___ but Thy grace can foil the tempt - er's pow'r?
Shine ___ thro' the gloom, and point me to the skies;

When ___ oth - er help - ers ___ fail, and com - forts flee,
Change ___ and de - cay in ___ all a - round I see;
Who, ___ like Thy - self, my ___ guide and stay can be?
Heav'n's ___ morn - ing breaks, and ___ earth's vain shad - ows flee!

Help of the help - less, oh, a - bide with me!
O Thou, who change-est not, a - bide with me!
Thro clouds and sun - shine, oh, a - bide with me!
In life, in death O, Lord, a - bide with me!

Star Gleams

For There Shall Be No More Night
MEMORIAL

C. B. J.

CARRIE BAXTER JENNINGS

Be - yond the smil-ing and the weep-ing They have found rest; The
It mat-ters not if streets are gold-en, Jas-per the walls, If

Mas - ter hath them in His keep-ing He know-eth best. No
harps in ser-aph hands be hold-en When Je-sus calls. For

more shall pain and grief be-cloud them For God Him-self shall be the light, And
them e-ter-nal day is break-ing In realms that are for-ev-er bright, For

nev - er-more shall dark-ness shroud them, For there shall be no more night.
them no sleep-ing and no wak-ing, For there shall be no more night.

Choice Note

Star Beams

Music "You May Have The Joy-bells"
Copyright, 1899, by Wm J. Kirkpatrick
Used by permission

CARRIE B. JENNINGS

W. J. KIRKPATRICK

1. Just a song of glad - ness, Just a ray of cheer,
2. Ban - ish strife and en - vy, ban - ish doubt and gloom.

bring - ing joy to loy - al hearts as - sem - bled ___ here;
Let no care find en - trance to our chap - ter ___ room;

While we greet our East - ern Star Let no note of sad - ness mar;
Hap - py hearts and voic - es raise, Greet with songs of lof - ty praise

Keep the lov - ing Star beams sing - ing in the heart
Him who keeps the Star beams sing - ing in the heart

Star Gleams

CHORUS

Star - - - - beams light - ing ev - ery mile,
Light - ing ev - ery mile

Star - - - - beams glow - ing all the while;
Glow - ing all the while

If their pre - cepts we o - bey They will light us all the way;

Joy - ous, lov - ing Star - beams Shin - ing in the heart.

Star Gleams

Happy Greeting To All

Re-adapted by CARRIE B. JENNINGS

Allegretto

1. Come, sis-ters, and join in our fes-ti-val song, And hail the sweet
2. In one fes-tal song let our voic-es re-sound, Let peace and good
3. Our Fa-ther in heav-en, we lift up to Thee Our voice of thanks-

joys which this day brings a-long, We'll join our glad voic-es in
will in our or-der a-bound Let har-mo-ny reign and no
giv-ing our glad ju-bi-lee; Oh grant that our la-bor of

one hymn of praise, To God who has kept us, and length-ened our days.
self-ish act mar The hour we de-vote to our bright East-ern Star
love be in-creased, For thus shall we hon-or our Star of the East

CHORUS

Hap-py greet-ing to all! Hap-py greet-ing to all!

Hap-py greet-ing to all!

Hap-py greet-ing, hap-py greet-ing, hap-py greet-ing to all!

Star Gleams

All Together

Adapted by C. B. J.

1. All to-geth-er, all to-geth-er, Once, once a-gain;
   While the East-ern Star is shin-ing Bright on our way

2. All to-geth-er, all to-geth-er, Joy-ful we sing;
   Ev-'ry cloud has sil-ver lin-ing, Storms can-not last;

Hearts and voic-es__ light as ev-er, Glad-ly join the wel-come strain.
Let no thought of__ dull re-pin-ing Cast a shad-ow o'er the day,
Reck we naught of__ wind or weath-er, Loud-ly let the wel-kin ring
Where the East-ern__ Star is shin-ing There our hopes are an-chored fast,

CHORUS 2d time pp

O may we ev-er Dwell in peace and har-mo-ny

And each en-deav-or strength-en our fra-ter-ni-ty.

Star Gleams

Bethlehem

Tune_Galilee

DUET for SOPRANO and ALTO or TENOR and BARITONE

CARRIE B. JENNINGS

Oh love - ly night,———— oh peace - ful scene,———— A ten - der
And fair up - on———— the robe of night———— A sin - gle

moon,———— a sky se - rene———— And hark! the
star———— in vades the sight,———— And lo, the

her - - - ald an - gels sing———— And loud and
wise———— men from a - far———— Be - hold and

Star Gleams

ring.
Star.
clear their an - thems ring, their an - thems ring.
fol - - - low Beth - l'em's, fol - low Beth - l'em's Star.
Oh Beth - le - hem to thee we bring Glad
Oh won - drous Star, fair Beth - l'em's Star, No
tid - ings of a new - born King; No prov - ince shall thy
oth - er light shall shine so far; And ne'er shall be so
rit.
name con - temn Oh, lit - tle, lit - tle town of Beth - le - hem.
pure a gem As that, as that bright Star of Beth - le - hem.
lit rall. tle
that bright

Chant for O. E. S. Initiatory Work

Arranged by Mrs. Nettie Ransford, Grand Secretary Indiana, and Past Most Worthy Grand Matron O.E.S.

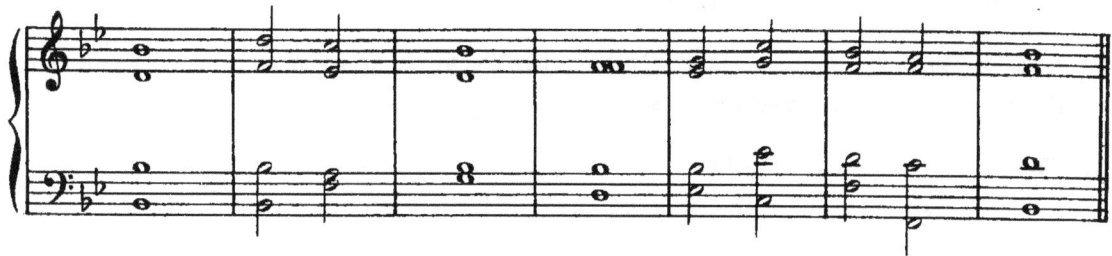

During march following obligation

1. Happy is the man that | find-eth | Wisdom: | and the man that | get-teth | un-der- | standing.

2. She is more | precious than | rubies: | and all the things thou canst desire are not | to be com- | par-ed | un-to | her.

3. Her ways are | ways of | pleasantness and | all her | paths are | peace.

Between first and second points

1. And Jephthah came to Mizpah un- | to his | house: | and behold his daughter came forth to meet him with | tim- brels | and with | dances.

2. And she was his | on-ly | child: | beside her he had | nei-ther | son nor | daughter.

3. And it came to pass, when he saw her, that he rent his clothes and said, "A- | las my| daughter: | thou hast | brought me | ver-y | low."

4. And thou art one of them that | trou-ble | me: | for I have opened my mouth unto the Lord and I | can-not | go-| back.

Between second and third points

1. And behold, Boaz came from Bethlehem and said unto the reapers, "The | Lord be | with you": | and they answered him "The| Lord | bless | thee."

2. Then said Boaz | unto his | servant that was set over the reapers | "Whose| damsel| is | this?"

3. And the servant that was set over the reapers | answered and | said: | "It is the Moabitish damsel that came back with Naomi| out of the | country of | Moab."

Star Gleams

Between third and fourth points

1. And it was so, when the king saw Esther the queen | standing in the | court | that she obtained | fa-vor | in his|sight.

2. And the king held out to Esther the golden scepter that was | in his | hand: | so Esther drew near and | touched the | top of the | scepter.

3. Then said the king unto her, "What wilt thou, Queen Esther? and what is | thy re- | quest? | "It shall be given thee to the | half | of the | kingdom."

Between fourth and fifth points

1. Then said Martha unto Jesus, "Lord, if thou hadst been here my brother | had not | died: | but I know that even now whatsoever thou wilt ask of God | God will | give it | thee."

2. Jesus saith unto her, "Thy brother shall | rise a- | gain." | Martha saith unto him "I know that he shall rise again in the resurrection | at the | last | day."

3. Jesus saith unto her "I am the ressurection and the life, he that believeth in me, though he were dead, yet | shall he | live, | and whosoever liveth and believeth in| me shall | nev-er | die."

Following fifth lecture

1. W. P. "Grace be | with | you, | mercy, and | peace, from | God the | Father."

2. "And now I beseech thee, lady, not as though I wrote a new commandment | un-to thee, | but that which we had from the beginning, that we | love | one an- | other."

3. "And | this is | love, | that we walk | af-ter | His com- | mandments."

4. "By this we know that we walk | in the | truth. | Behold what manner of love the Father| hath be- | stowed up- |on us."

5. "That we should be called the| children of | God. | That our | joy may| be| full."

6. "Beloved, let us love one another, for love | is of | God, | and every one that loveth and knoweth | God, is | born of | God."

7. "Herein is love, not that we loved God, but that he | first loved | us. | If God so loved us, we ought | also to | love one | another."

Crossing The Bar

ALFRED TENNYSON

CARRIE B. JENNINGS

Sun - set and eve - ning star And one clear call for

me, And may there be no moan - ing of the bar When

I put out to sea But such a tide as mov - ing

seems a - sleep, Too full for sound and foam When

that which drew from out the bound-less deep Turns a - gain home.

Twi - light and eve - ning bell And af - ter that the dark And

may there be no sad - ness of fare - well When I em - bark For

though from out our bourne of time and place The flood may bear me far___ I

me far

hope to see my pi - lot face to face When I have

crossed When I have crossed the bar. A - men.

Crossing 2

There are Stars Above that Softly Shimmer

MIXED VOICES

By CARRIE BAXTER JENNINGS

Piano

There are stars a-bove that soft-ly shim-mer, In the
All a-long life's path-way lights are gleam-ing, Lest un-

fir - ma-ment of blue, There are twink - ling stars whose sil - v'ry
wa - ry feet should stray; Shad - ows oft of sub-stance have the

glim-mer, O'er the fields of night fair blos-soms strew;____ There are
seem-ing Daz-zled by the gar-ish light of day;____ Let us

Mixed V. - 2

stars in myr-i-ads that clus-ter, Like a spray of in-can-des-cent spar,— But the
in fra-ter-nal love a-bid-ing, By the bea-con bright that shines a-far,— Shape our

star that shines with pur-est lus-ter, Is our glo-ri-ous East-ern Star.—
course and trust un-to the guid-ing, Of our glo-ri-ous East-ern Star.—

OSSIA

lus-ter, Is our glo-ri-ous East-ern Star.—
guid-ing, Of our glo-ri-ous East-ern Star.—

OPENING
In Chapter Assembled
Tune: "Sweet Afton"

CARRIE B. JENNINGS

In chap-ter as-sem-bled a - gain we u - nite With hands that are will-ing and
Our Fa-ther in Heav-en we hum-bly im-plore Thy bless-ing, be-stow on our

hearts tuned a - right, Our la-bors fra - ter - nal a - gain to re - sume, At
chap - ter once more, Be with us and guide us in all that we do, And

home in the realm of our lov'd chap-ter room. Our Star in the East shines so
sanc-tion the pledg-es that here we re - new. The steps may we fol - low with

lus-trous and clear, A sym-bol of per-fect love cast-ing out fear. All doubts are dis -
pur-pose new-born, Of those whose life les-sons our or-der a-dorn, Nor fail to re -

pelled and our voic-es we raise In thanks to the pow'r that has length-ened our days.
flect where-so - ev-er we are The pre-cepts and light of our bright East-ern Star.

Star Gleams

Keep The Watch Fires Burning

Rallying Song

Written for Montcalm - Mecosta Association 1920

CARRIE B. JENNINGS

Mrs. Ivah Larry, President.

Old Camp Meeting Air

Lively

1 Daugh-ters of the East-ern Star, Keep the watch-fires burn-ing, burn-ing,
2 Daugh-ters of the East-ern Star, Keep the watch-fires glow-ing, glow-ing,
3 Daugh-ters of the East-ern Star, Keep the watch-fires gleam-ing, gleam-ing,

Fine

Let the bea-con shine a-far, Our glo-rious or-der dis-cern-ing;
In the cor-ner where you are A wealth of sis-'ter-hood show-ing;
Send the bea-con light a-far, With rays of sis-ter-ly mean-ing;

Join then a song of praise, Loud-ly your voic-es raise,
Let not your ar-dor lag, Let not your cour-age flag,
Keep aye the watch-fires bright All thro the dark-est night,

D.C. al Fine

Prov-ing in wis-dom's ways The beau-ties of our or-der.
Float from each hill and crag The ban-ner of our or-der.
Trust to their guid-ing light Some ship-wrecked life's re-deem-ing.

Star Gleams

OPENING or CLOSING
Soft Light and Tender
Tune:"Juanita"

C. B. JENNINGS

Mixed Voices

Andante

mf

Soft light and ten-der Break-ing thru the glooms that low'r, Gleam - ing in
Once more to geth-er 'Neath our Star's fra-ter-nal rays, Pray - ing our

mf

splen-dor In this gra-cious hour. Rend-ing clouds of sad-ness, Turn-ing dark-ness
Fa-ther Guide and keep our ways. Make us all for-giv-ing, Each the oth-ers

in - to day, Shed-ding light and glad-ness On our pil-grim way.
bur-den share, Trust-ing, work-ing, liv-ing, In His watch-ful care.

mf a tempo

Shin-ing, ev - er shin-ing, Send-ing beams of love a - far,
Shin-ing, fad - ing nev - er, Our bright Star our guide shall be,

mf a tempo

Day's dawn or de - clin - ing Greets our East-ern Star.
Shin-ing, gleam - ing ev - er Thru E - ter - ni - ty.

Star Gleams

ONCE MORE IN FRATERNAL LOVE BLENDING

BY

CARRIE BAXTER JENNINGS

Written for the Montcalm-Mecosta County Association 1922; Mrs. Mattie E. Horton, President.

Tune —"Columbia The Gem of The Ocean"
Page 10 Star Gleams

Once more in fraternal love blending
  Our voices in chorus resound
In thanks for a care never ending
  And mercies which ever abound.
For the hand that has kept and protected,
  For the glory that shineth afar,
For the light of true purpose reflected
  In the rays of our bright Eastern Star,
  In the rays of our bright Eastern Star,
  In the rays of our bright Eastern Star,
For the light of true purpose reflected
  In the rays of our bright Eastern Star.

May the bonds of fraternal love ever
  The ranks of our order unite,
And naught ever tend to dissever
  Or discord and envy incite.
May the light of our Star streaming o'er us
  Thru our lives glow with beauty afar,
With her flag proudly floating before us
  Sound the praise of our bright Eastern
    Star,
  Sound the praise of our bright Eastern
    Star,
  Sound the praise of our bright Eastern
    Star,
With her flag proudly floating before us
  Sound the praise of our bright Eastern
    Star.

OUR STAR IS SHINING ON

BY

CARRIE BAXTER JENNINGS

Written in honor of Miss Irene Louise Getty, W. G. M., and Mrs. Ada C. Sangster. A. G. M., O. E. S., Mich., May 16, 1922

Tune — "Battle Hymn of The Republic"
Page 6 Star Gleams

I fain would sing the praises of our glorious
  Eastern Star;
I would tell in song and story what its in-
  spirations are;
I would write its name in letters that should
  send its fame afar;
  Our Star is shining on.

CHORUS

Glory, Glory, hallelujah, glory, glory,
  hallelujah;
Glory, glory, hallelujah, Our Star is Shin-
  ing on.

All should know its chosen symbol is The
  Star of Bethlehem
Which adown thru all the ages shines a
  pure and priceless gem;
It is worthy of a setting in a royal diadem,
  Our Star is shining on.

I would tell the world its mission to the
  widow in her need;
To protect the friendless orphan as a friend
  in truth and deed;
Of succor for the aged, all its worthiness
  I'd plead;
  Our Star is shining on.

Then let us sound its praises, let them ring
  o'er vale and hill;
Let the echoes keep resounding till our
  songs the welkin fill;
Let us shout the joyful tidings, that our
  Star is shining still;
  Our Star is shining on.

Star Gleams

"Now The Day Is Over"

Adapted by request for O. E. S. Closing Ode.

CARRIE B. JENNINGS   JOSEPH BARNBY

Now the day is o - ver   Once a - gain we
In the path be - fore us   Tri - als may be -
Bless the star we fol - low   Bless this clos - ing

part_____   Sav - iour, let thy bless - ing
fall_____   But thy lov - ing kind - ness
hour_____   Keep us and sus - tain us

bless - ing rest on
kind - ness watch - es
hold us by Thy

Rest on ev - 'ry heart
Watch - es o - ver all
By Thy right - hand's pow'r   A - men

ev - - ry heart
o - - ver all
right - - hand's pow'r

www.ingramcontent.com/pod-product-compliance
Lightning Source LLC
Chambersburg PA
CBHW081650270326
41933CB00018B/3424